My First Picture Dictionary

Illustrated by
ALBIN STĂNESCU

Brown Watson (Leicester) Ltd

My First Picture Dictionary

Illustrated by
ALBIN STĂNESCU

Published by

Brown Watson (Leicester) Ltd

Children's Book Publishers

55A, London Road, Leicester LE2 OPE

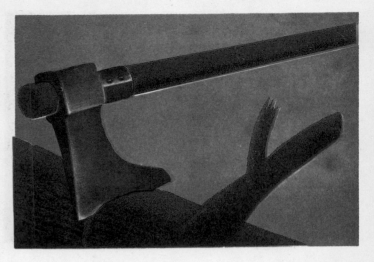

AXE A sharp edged tool used for cutting down trees.

APPLE A delicious fresh fruit grown in many parts of the world.

AQUARIUM A place to keep and view fish and underwater plants.

AIRPORT This is a terminus for aeroplanes to land and take off from.

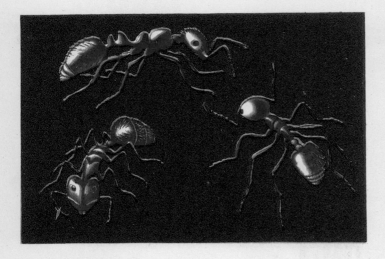

ANTS Small insects particularly noted for their industrious and workmanlike ways.

APRON A pretty piece of material worn over the front of the body to keep your other clothes clean.

AEROPLANE These can fly very high and take people to many parts of the world.

A.B.C. A simple beginners' book for children learning to read.

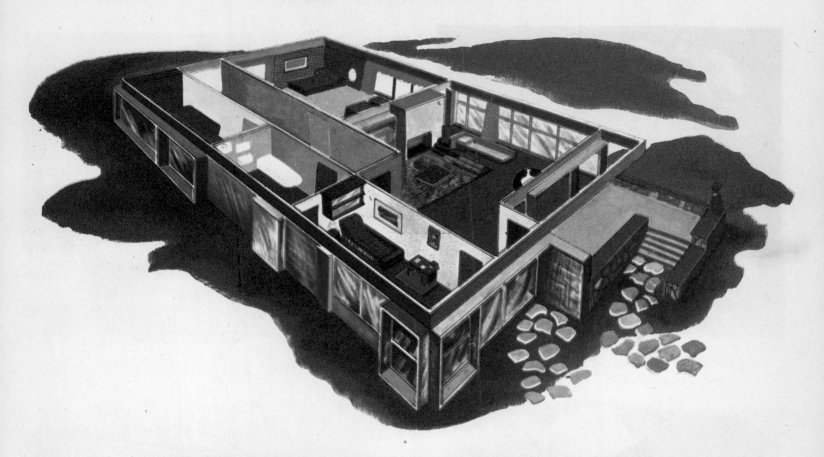

APARTMENT A term sometimes used to describe a flat or rooms.

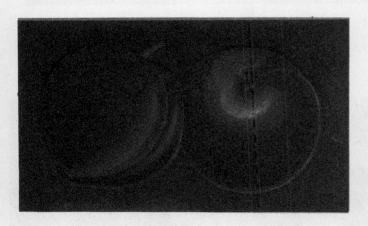

APRICOT An orange-coloured, soft, hard-stoned fruit.

AUTUMN The season between summer and winter when the harvest is gathered.

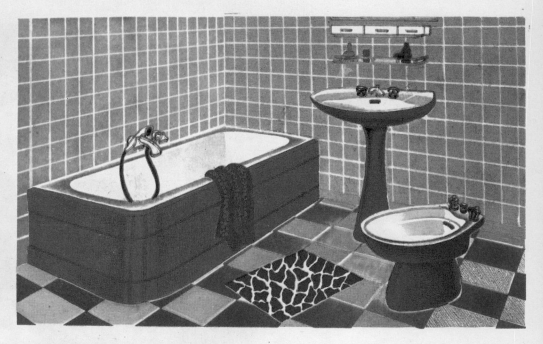

BATHROOM This is the room where you go to have a bath or wash your hands and face.

BAKER He is the man who makes bread. He also bakes cakes.

BOOTS Fur-lined boots like those shown are nice to wear when the weather is cold or it is snowing.

BEAR Bears love honey. They steal it from hives to eat.

BUFFALO The buffalo is a very large kind of ox. They used to be hunted for their meat and skins.

BILBERRY A plant that yields a sweet tasting, purple berry.

BEE Bees collect pollen from the flowers and then take it back to their hives to make honey.

BRICKLAYER This man's skill with bricks helps to build houses.

BED At night time, when you are tired, you go to bed to sleep.

BEECH TREE This tree has a very smooth bark and its leaves are oval-shaped.

BRIDGE Bridges carry cars and trains across gaps like rivers.

BICYCLE Bicycles are fun to ride. You can pedal very fast on them.

BEETLE The beetle is an insect that destroys leaves and plants by slowly eating away at them.

BOTANICAL GARDENS These are beautiful gardens that house all the many kinds of plant life that grow throughout the world.

BLACK BIRD This bird is a dark-coloured species of thrush. They like to pull out worms from the ground and eat them.

BOOK SHELF You use this to keep your collection of books nice and tidy. Your Picture Dictionary should be kept there, too.

BULL The bull is the mate to a cow and the father of calves.

BALLOONS Balloons are brightly coloured and when they are filled with air, they float.

BLACKBERRY This is a small berry that grows on the bramble and can be eaten as a fruit.

BRICKS These are blocks of clay baked hard and used as a building stone.

BUTTERFLY These are beautifully coloured insects that start life as caterpillars.

BEDROOM Your bed is kept in this room. You should also have cupboards and a wardrobe to keep your clothes in.

BOOK Some books, like your Picture Dictionary, are full of information. Others, like the one in the picture, have fairy tales for you to read.

BOAT There are many different kinds of boats. The one in the picture is called a rowing boat.

CABIN People who go to stay in the mountains live in houses called cabins.

CLOCK We need clocks to tell us the time of day. The one shown tells us that it is ten minutes past nine.

COOKING Most food has to be cooked before it can be eaten. Is your Mummy a good cook?

CAR There are many types of car. The one in the picture is a sports car and can go very fast.

CUP A cup is used for drinking from. Most people drink tea or coffee from them.

CLASSROOM When you go to school, you sit in a classroom with your friends to learn your lessons.

COACH People go for coach rides to visit places. They can carry lots of people.

CARPENTER Carpenters work with wood. They use tools like hammers, saws, chisels and screwdrivers.

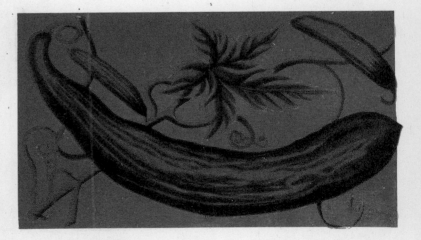

CUCUMBER Although the cucumber is a fruit, they are mostly eaten in salads. They are green in colour.

CHICK A chick is a young bird. They are all fluffy when they are hatched.

CARROT Carrots are actually roots of a plant. We eat them as a vegetable.

CABBAGE This is a vegetable, too. The centre of a cabbage is known as the heart.

CRANE Cranes are used for lifting very heavy loads. A man, sitting in a cabin at the top, operates the crane.

CHERRIES Cherries are a sweet fruit with a little stone in the centre of them.

COW We get our milk from cows. Can you see her udders?

CAMEL The camel lives in hot climates like the Sahara Desert. It can go for many days without water.

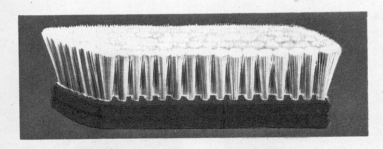

CLOTHES BRUSH This brush has lots of bristles. They help to keep your clothes clean.

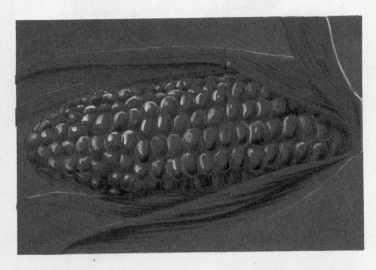

CORN Corn is grown and used as a cereal. Do you like cornflakes for breakfast?

COMB By running the teeth of a comb through your hair, you can keep it tidy.

COAT This is a garment worn over your clothes to keep you warm.

CART In some countries, farmers use carts drawn by oxen to move heavy loads.

CROCODILE This reptile can live on land or in water. His sharp teeth make him very dangerous.

CUPBOARDS Cupboards are used for **storing** things away in.

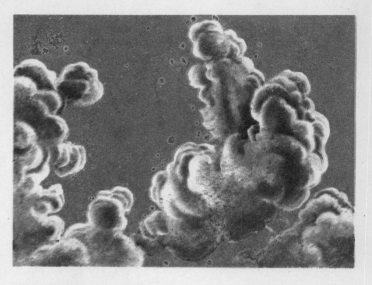

CLOUDS Clouds in the sky usually mean **rain**. They are visible masses of water vapour.

COMBINED HARVESTER This machine reaps and threshes corn or wheat at the same time.

COCK This is the male bird. His crowing heralds the dawn.

CUCKOO The cuckoo is a funny bird. She lays her eggs in other birds' nests.

CAKE There are many delicious varieties of cake. Do you like to eat some for your tea?

CLOWNS You see clowns at circuses. They wear funny clothes and have painted faces.

CINEMA Films are shown at cinemas. The one in our picture is called a cartoon.

CALF A calf is a baby cow or bull. They are very tiny when they are born.

CEMENT MIXER The round bowl part of this machine mixes sand, water and powdered cement into the substance used for building.

COSMOS The sun, the moon, the stars and the planets; the Universe as a whole is known as the Cosmos.

CARPET Carpets are used as floor coverings. They are made out of different materials like wool or nylon.

17

DAHLIA Dahlias are very pretty and have single and double flowers.

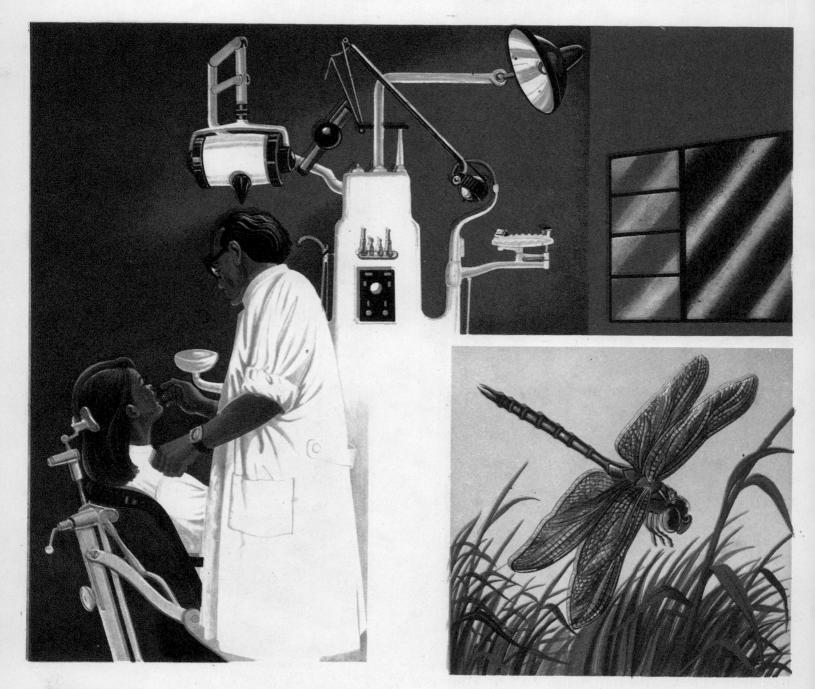

DENTIST When your teeth ache, the dentist is the man who looks after them.

DRAGONFLY This insect has a very long body and huge wings.

DONKEY Donkeys are beasts of burden. They are used for giving children rides at the seaside as well.

DOLL Dolls are nice toys to have. They can be dressed up in many different outfits.

DEER In bygone days, the deer was hunted for its meat.

DRESS A dress is a long garment worn by women.

DOLPHINS These are very intelligent and playful fish. They can be trained to do many clever tricks.

DOG Dogs are known as 'man's best friend'. They make very good pets.

EDUCATION Being educated can mean everything from learning arithmetic, geography and history to being taught how to play games.

ELEPHANT This powerful animal can be found mostly in the jungles of Africa and India.

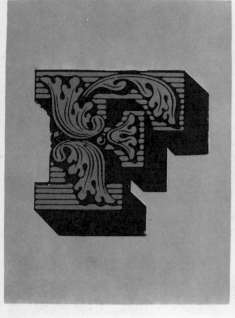

FACTORY A factory is a workshop for making or manufacturing goods.

FLAMINGO Look at the long legs and beaks these beautiful birds have. They also have scarlet feathers.

FLOWERS There are many kinds of flowers. How many can you spot in the picture?

FLAX This plant is cultivated for its textile fibre.

FORK A fork has a long handle and four prongs at the end. This is to help you pick up your food when eating.

FROG Frogs can live on land or in water. They move by hopping.

FLATS A block of flats is lots of small houses built on top of one another.

FLAG Each country has a flag with its national colours on. The flag in the picture represents Romania.

FROGMAN With special breathing equipment, frogmen can stay underwater for a long time.

FARM The farm in the picture is a dairy farm. Cows are kept there for their milk.

FAIRY TALES Fairy tales are make-believe stories about mythical people and lands.

FOX This is a cunning animal. They like to eat the farmer's chickens.

GLASS Glasses are drinking vessels. This glass has orange juice in it.

GIRAFFE Do you see the giraffe's long legs and neck? This is so that it can reach up to the tall branches and eat the leaves off the trees.

GERANIUM Although the geranium is a wild plant, they can also be grown indoors.

GARDENER He is the man who tends the garden. He keeps it looking very pretty by weeding and pruning.

GRAPES Grapes are eaten as a fruit. They grow on vines. Wine is also made from them.

GOAT The goat in the picture is a black goat. He likes to run free in rocky surrounds.

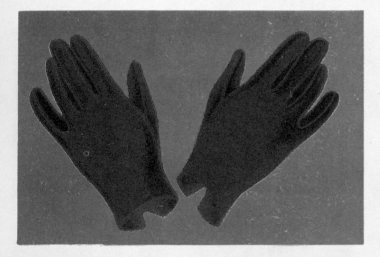

GLOVES Gloves are shaped like hands. This is so that your fingers can fit snugly into them.

GRASS This green vegetation is the staple diet for many animals.

GAZELLE The gazelle is a graceful, soft-eyed kind of antelope.

GOAT Here is another kind of goat. See how long and shaggy his coat is.

GARLIC Garlic is used as a flavouring in cooking. It has a very strong taste.

GROCERIES This is a collective term for food bought from the shops.

GOLDFINCH Our friend the goldfinch is a brightly-coloured song bird.

GAS STOVE Your Mummy cooks the food on a gas stove.

GATE If you have a fence or a wall surrounding a building, you need a gate to be able to go in and out.

HEMP The fibres of hemp are very tough and are used for making rope.

HAYSTACK After the hay has been cut, it is stacked as shown in the picture.

HEDGEHOG This tiny animal curls himself into a ball when he is in danger. The sharp spines on his back protect him.

HEN Most of us like eggs for breakfast. The hen lays them for us.

HYDRO-ELECTRICITY This is electricity produced by water power.

HORSE As well as a beast of burden the horse is used in sporting circles. The one in the picture is a race horse.

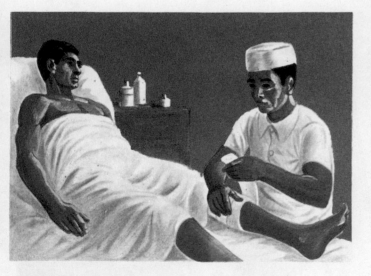

HOSPITAL Doctors and nurses work in hospitals. That is where people go when they are ill.

HOE This is a garden tool. It turns over the earth and digs up weeds.

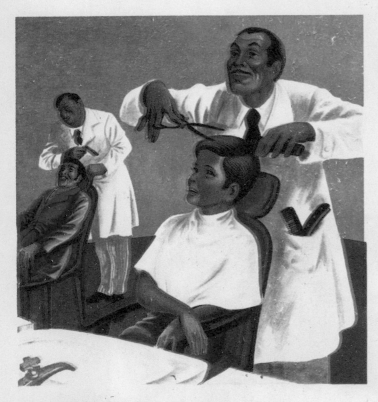

HOUSE Houses are dwellings for people to live in. They are usually made from bricks.

HAIRDRESSER Hairdressers cut and style hair. Have you had your hair cut recently?

HANDKERCHIEF These are square-shaped pieces of linen which we use to blow our noses on.

HARE Hares look a bit like rabbits, but they have longer legs. They can run very fast.

HATS Here are two different kinds of hats. The one on the left is fur-lined and is called a hunting hat. The one on the right is a trilby.

HIPPOPOTAMUS These are African animals which live in rivers.

ICE-CREAM You eat ice-cream when it has been chilled in the fridge. It comes in many flavours.

INSULAR This is an island surrounded on all sides by water.

JACKAL Jackals are animals of the dog kind. They are about the size of a fox.

JOCKEYS Men who ride horses in races are called jockeys.

KANGAROO This animal is a marsupial. This means it carries its young in a pouch.

KID This is the name given to a baby goat.

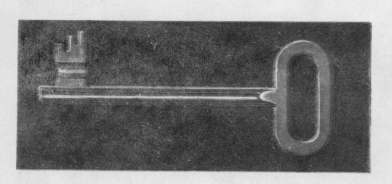

KEY To unlock a door or safe, you need a key. Each lock has its own key.

KITE Kites are brightly coloured pieces of material, tied to a piece of string, which soar high into the air carried by the wind.

LAKE Lakes are an expanse of water usually surrounded by highland.

LLAMAS They live in South America and are like the camel but without humps.

LEOPARD A variety of jungle cat, the leopard's distinguishing marks are its spots.

LINEN This is cloth woven from flax. Do you remember seeing the flax plant earlier in the book?

LIBRARY A library is a collection of books. It is also a building where you can go to borrow books.

LION The lion is a magnificent beast and is known as 'the King of the jungle'

LOCOMOTIVE This train is powered by overhead electric cables.

LINER This is a term given to a passenger-carrying cruise ship.

LIGHTNING Those zigzag flashes are caused by an electrical discharge between clouds.

LEMON This yellow fruit has a very bitter taste. Its juices are used in the making of lemonade.

LOCUST Locust are very destructive insects. They devour large areas of vegetation in their thousands.

LEAF Plants and trees have leaves. They are generally green and grow from out of the sides of stems and branches.

LADYBIRD A harmless insect, the ladybird is reddish-brown in colour and has black spots on its back.

LORRY A lorry is a large flat, sideless wagon. They can carry bulky or heavy loads.

LOUNGE Sometimes known as the sitting-room, the lounge is the main room of the house where the sofa and arm-chairs are kept.

LAMB This fluffy little animal is born in the spring and is the baby of the sheep.

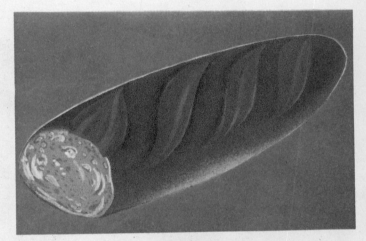

LOAF To make a loaf of bread you mix yeast, flour and water and then bake the mixture in an oven.

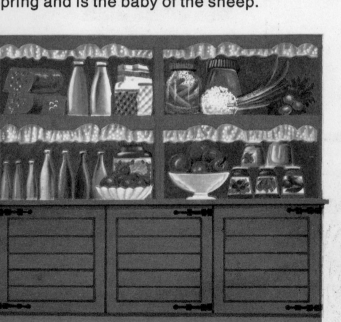

LARDER A larder is a cupboard or dresser in the kitchen where your Mummy stores the food.

LADLE A form of spoon, the ladle has a long handle and a large cup bowl so that large amounts of liquid can be served at one time.

LYNX These wild cats are noted for their short tails, spotted fur and tufted ear-tips.

MONKEY The monkey lives in trees. He is a creature that closely resembles man.

MIRROR Mirrors reflect our images. This enables us to look at ourselves like the little girl is doing.

MINK A semi-aquatic, stoat-like animal. The mink is killed for its fur, from which they make coats.

MONUMENT These are built to commemorate historical occasions or important events.

MOUSE The mouse is a member of the rodent family. They are shy and timid creatures.

MINE Mines are dug deep into the ground so that minerals like coal can be excavated.

MOUNTAIN Mountains reach high into the sky. It is very cold at the top of mountains and there is nearly always snow which caps the peaks.

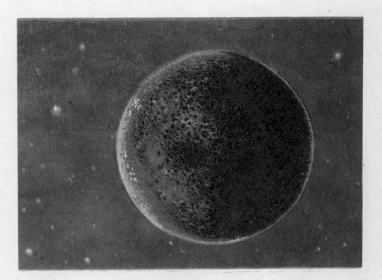

MOON The moon circles the earth once every twenty-four hours. It provides us with light in the sky at night.

MUG A mug is a large type of cup.

MILK Milk comes from the cow and is very nourishing to drink.

MELON This is a water melon. It is green on the outside and red inside. It has lots of large pips.

MALLARD This is a wild drake or duck.

MINER This is a man who works in a mine. He helps to dig the coal.

MUSHROOM Mushrooms are an edible fungus that grow wild in the countryside.

NEWSPAPERS Newspapers print and report the news.

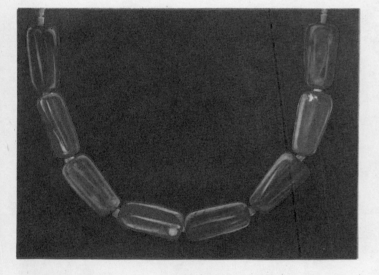

NECKLACE A necklace is made up of beads or pieces of jewellery threaded on to a piece of string and worn round the neck.

NUTS Nuts have hard outer shells to protect the fruit inside. The nuts in the picture are called walnuts.

NATIVITY The Nativity refers to the birth of Jesus which we celebrate at Christmas time.

OWL Owls are strange birds. They sleep in the day and fly at night.

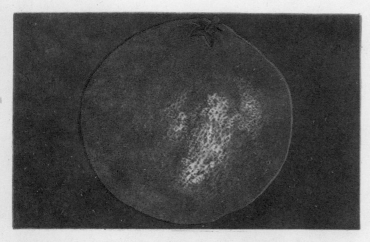

ORANGE This is a citrus fruit with a yellow-reddish tough rind. It has also given its name to the colour.

OATS Oats are grown and used as a cereal for humans and food for horses.

ORCHARD An orchard is the name given to a place which grows all kinds of fruit.

OASIS An oasis is a fertile spot in a desert where palm trees grow by a water hole.

OPERA An opera is a dramatic play set to music where the actors sing their lines.

OAK TREE These are tall, strong trees. The fruit of an oak tree is the acorn.

ONIONS These are edible bulbs which are used as flavouring in cooking.

47

OSTRICH This is a large African bird. It is said that the ostrich buries its head in the sand when it is in danger.

PARROT This bird has a beautifully coloured plumage. It can be taught to speak.

PAINTING A painting is a term given to pictures produced on canvas. They are framed and hung in galleries

PARACHUTE Parachutes are made from silk or nylon

PIGS Pigs are plump animals which are reared for their meat which is called pork. We also get bacon from pigs.

PLUMS A plum is a dark-coloured stoned fruit. When the plum is dried it is then known as a prune.

POPPY In the fields one can see lots of poppies.

PEPPERS These are very strong smelling and tasting plants used in cooking, either as a flavouring or as a vegetable.

PLATE Plates come in all different sizes. We eat food off plates.

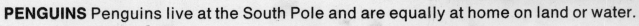

PENGUINS Penguins live at the South Pole and are equally at home on land or water.

POSTMAN The postman delivers letters, cards and parcels to people.

PEAR The pear is a fruit. It is large at the bottom and tapers to the stalk.

PINE TREE Pine trees are evergreens. This means that they have green leaves all the year round.

PELICAN Pelicans are fish eaters. They catch fish and store them in their pouch under their beaks.

51

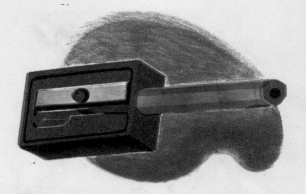

PENCIL SHARPENER This is a small 'box' with a very sharp blade on top. By putting a blunt pencil in at the open end and turning it, the blade sharpens it to a point.

POTATOES These are plant tubers which are cooked in many different ways and used as food.

PIANO This is a musical instrument. Its keys are made of ivory.

PARK A park is an enclosed expanse of grass and trees. They are very pleasant places to visit.

PENCIL A pencil is a long piece of lead encased by wood. By making a point to the lead you can draw or write with it.

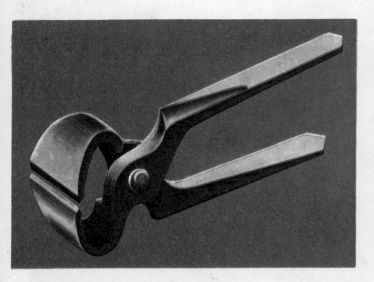

PLIERS This tool is used to bend wire with or pull out old nails from wood.

PINE This is what we call the 'leaves' of the pine tree. They are needle shaped.

PIGEON Pigeons can be wild or domesticated birds. Some people keep them and use them to race against one another.

QUEEN A queen is the Crowned Ruler of a country.

QUAIL This bird is allied to the partridge and is thought very highly of as food.

QUAY A landing place for unloading ships.

RAILWAY STATION Trains pull into stations so that passengers can get on and off them. The passengers stand on a platform.

RADIATORS Hot water flows through radiators which in turn throw out heat to help warm rooms.

RADISHES These are roots which are eaten raw, often in salads.

RAINBOW Rainbows are the result of the sun's rays reflecting in falling drops of rain and are made up of seven colours.

RASPBERRIES Raspberries are the red fruit of its plant and can be eaten or made into jam.

RUBBER A rubber, or eraser, is an implement used to wipe out mistakes when writing or drawing.

ROSE This is a sweet-smelling flower which grows on bushes whose stems are covered with thorns.

RADIO The radio in the picture is used to receive programmes broadcasted by a radio station.

RIVER Rivers usually begin in the mountains and flow down to the sea.

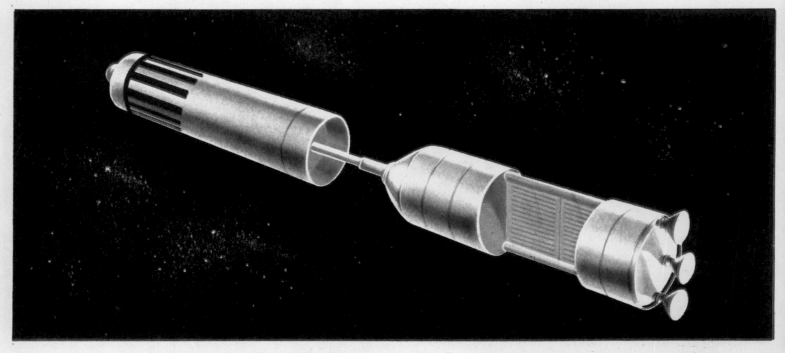

ROCKET Rockets are launched into space to carry men or scientific instruments for research purposes..

STOATS Stoat is the general name for ermine. Other animals in this family include the weasel and ferret.

SWANS The swan is a graceful water-bird. Look at its long neck and magnificent plumage.

SAW A saw has sharp, jagged teeth to enable you to cut wood.

SNAKE Snakes are of the reptile family. Some snakes are very poisonous. The danger is in the snake's forked tongue.

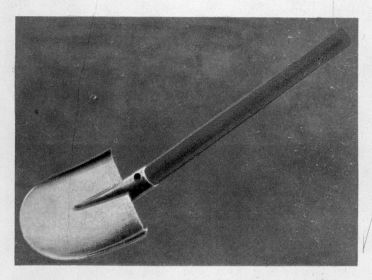

SPADE This is a hand tool for digging earth. It has a long wooden handle and a sharp-edged steel blade.

SUN The earth revolves around the sun. It supplies our planet with its light and warmth.

SQUIRREL Squirrels have long bushy tails and live in trees. They hibernate in winter.

SWIMMING POOL A swimming pool has a deep end and a shallow end. That is so everyone can enjoy swimming in safety.

SCISSORS Scissors have two sharp cutting edges. They are used mainly for cutting material.

SWALLOW These birds have forked tails and long wings. They are usually associated with summer.

SHARK The shark is the most dangerous of all fish, not only to other sea life but also to man.

SHOES Shoes are made from leather with rubber soles. We wear them on our feet.

SOAP We use soap to wash with. By rubbing in water you get a lather.

SHEEP The outer coat of the sheep is sheared and from it, garments such as jumpers are made. We call the sheep's coat wool.

SEWING A long pointed needle with an eye at one end is used for sewing. A piece of cotton is threaded through the eye.

STEELWORKER The steelworker watches the furnace to get top-quality steel.

SPECTACLES The glass in a pair of spectacles are called lenses which help people with poor eyesight to see better.

SCARF Usually made from wool or silk, the scarf is worn round the neck to help keep you warm.

SHOE MENDERS Soles and heels on shoes wear down and they have to be repaired. The shoe mender does just that.

SATCHEL A satchel is a leather case carried on your back. School children use one to carry their books to school.

SWEETS This is a collective term used to describe a form of confectionary. Sweets can be many delicious things like chocolate, toffee, fudge and mint.

SLIDE A slide is a slippery surface which starts quite high off the ground and slopes back down.

SNOWMAN Snowmen are made by rolling snow up into a big ball and then left to freeze. A face is made by using buttons for his eyes and, like in the picture, a carrot for his nose.

STAG The stag is the male of the red deer and is distinguished by his magnificent antlers.

SPIDER Spiders live in webs which they spin themselves. They use the web to trap other insects, like flies, which they eat.

STORK The stork is a wading bird. Sometimes he stands in the water for hours on just one leg.

STORM A storm is heavy rain accompanied by thunder and lightning. When it snows very heavily we call this a snow storm.

SAND Rocks continually washed by sea water, or subjected to vast changes of temperature, slowly crumble to a powder that we call sand.

SCALES These are used to find out how much things weigh. The scales in the picture would be used in a grocer's shop for weighing food.

SUNFLOWER With its golden-rayed flowers, you can see why this is called a sunflower.

SHOP Shops are places where you go to buy things. There are many different shops selling different products.

STRAWBERRIES Grown on bushes, this fruit is red in colour. They are a summer fruit.

SANDALS These are open shoes fastened by straps. They are worn mainly in summer.

SKYLARK This lovely bird likes to fly spirally upwards singing.

STATUE A statue is a cast or moulded figure of someone . . . usually famous.

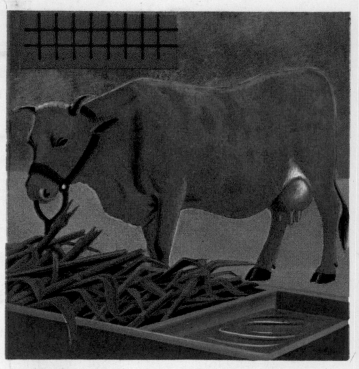

STABLE Animals like cows are kept in stables, particularly in winter. This is so that farmers can make sure that they are safe.

SHIRT Made from many different materials, shirts are garments worn mainly by men. They have a collar and cuffs and are fastened by buttons running right down the front.

SNAIL This very slow moving insect carries its house on its back.

SLEDGE Sledges are flat surfaces mounted on metal runners. These enable them to run freely over snow.

SATELLITE Satellites circle the earth sending back information to scientists. They can also be used to relay television pictures from countries many thousands of miles apart.

SOLDIER A soldier is a single member of an army. They carry guns and other weapons.

STONES This is a general term used to describe pieces of rock which can come in any size.

SPARROW This chirpy bird is very common indeed. They are plainly coloured. You can see lots of sparrows in your garden.

STAIRS Stairs are built to help us reach higher levels in our house.

SILVER BIRCH This tree is so called because they have two silver lines on the underside of their leaves.

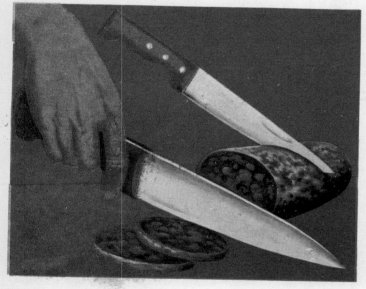

SALAMI This is an Italian sausage and is highly flavoured.

SANTA CLAUS We also know him as Father Christmas. He brings your presents at Christmas time.

SAILOR The sailor is a single member of a navy. They sail the sea in ships.

SNOWDROP This is a white coloured flower which appears in the spring.

SPOONS The spoon on the left is called a table spoon. This is usually used as a measure in cooking. The other one is a dessert spoon and we use it for eating our soup or afters with.

SEWING MACHINE Powered by an electric motor, this machine sends a needle with cotton threaded in it up and down very fast. By moving material underneath the needle, large areas can be sewn very quickly.

SWING A swing is a flat surface attached by rope or chains to a frame. By sitting on the swing and moving backwards and forwards you can swing to and fro and sometimes go very high into the air.

SOCKS You wear socks on your feet. They are made from wool or nylon.

STOOL This is a backless chair and is usually not very high off the ground.

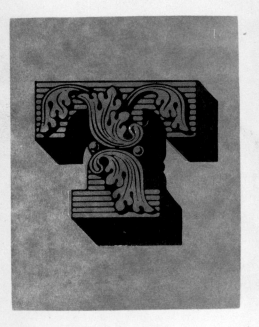

TEAL This is a kind of dark coloured, freshwater duck.

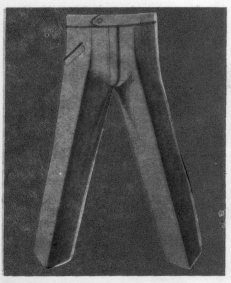

TROUSERS These are two-legged outer garments worn mostly by men.

TAILOR A tailor makes clothes. First he takes your measurements, then he marks them out on some material. Next he cuts the material and sews it up to the correct shape.

TWILIGHT This is the part of the day when the sun is setting and the moon is rising.

TRAM This is a sort of bus powered by overhead cables.

TRAFFIC LIGHTS The colours of traffic lights are red, amber and green. Each colour issues instructions to tell drivers what to do next.

TOWEL Towels are made from absorbant materials so that you can dry yourself on them after you have had a wash.

TELEVISION Programmes are broadcasted from television studios and the TV sets which are in our homes pick up the programmes for us to watch.

TELEPHONE People who own a telephone have a special number. When someone dials that number, your phone rings and by listening at the 'phone's earpiece you can hear the person talking. At the other end of the receiver is a mouthpiece which you use to speak back.

TABLE A flat-topped surface on legs. We sit at a table when we are having our dinner.

TRACTOR This is a farm vehicle which is used to pull heavy loads with.

TIGER Tigers are striped, ferocious jungle cats usually found in India.

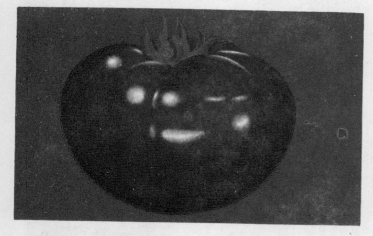

TOMATO A red-skinned, edible fruit, tomatoes are used as a vegetable. You can eat them cooked or raw.

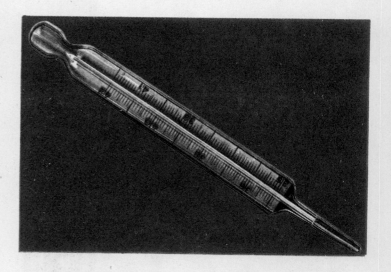

THERMOMETER A gauge for measuring the temperature. This is achieved by a line of mercury moving up and down the thermometer. It goes up when it is hot and moves down when it cools.

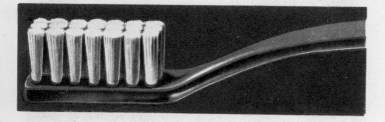

TOOTHBRUSH A small brush with stiff bristles and a long handle. You use this to brush your teeth with.

UMBRELLA Umbrellas are used to help keep us dry when it rains.

UNDERGROUND RAILWAY This is a network of tunnels which carry passenger trains across some large cities. We call the trains 'tubes.'

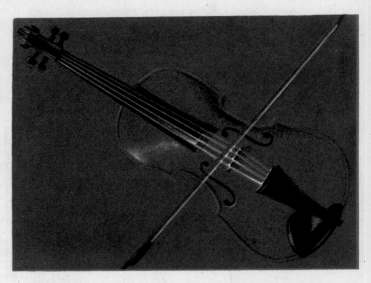

VIOLIN A musical instrument whose strings are made from cat gut. It is played by moving a bow across the strings.

VULTURE These are large birds of prey that feed mainly on dead animals.

WASHING MACHINE This is an automatic machine which washes, rinses and spins clothes dry.

WARDROBE A sort of cupboard used for hanging up your clothes in. Do you have one in your bedroom?

WASH BASIN This is bowl shaped with a hole at the bottom. To fill the basin you put a plug in the hole, and turn on the taps to allow water to flow into the bowl.

WOLVES Wolves hunt in packs. They prey mainly on sheep.

WINTER TIME This is the time of year when the trees are bare; the forest animals are hibernating and the ground is covered with snow.

WILLOWS These trees grow by the waterside and their branches and leaves droop towards the water. They are known as weeping willows.

WINDOW Made of glass and set in frames, windows help give rooms light and also allow us to look outside.

WELL This is a water well. The water is drawn from the well by a bucket tied onto a long piece of rope.

WASP This insect has black and yellow stripes, a slender body and a very nasty sting.

WHALE These large sea mammals are hunted for their oils and bones.

WELLINGTONS Wellington boots are made from rubber or plastic and are worn to protect feet from water.

WOODPECKER This bird taps the bark of the tree with its beak to discover insects.

WHEAT The seed of wheat is very nutritious and can be eaten when refined.

WATERING CAN Can you see the water spraying out of the spout? This is so that plants can be watered gently and evenly.

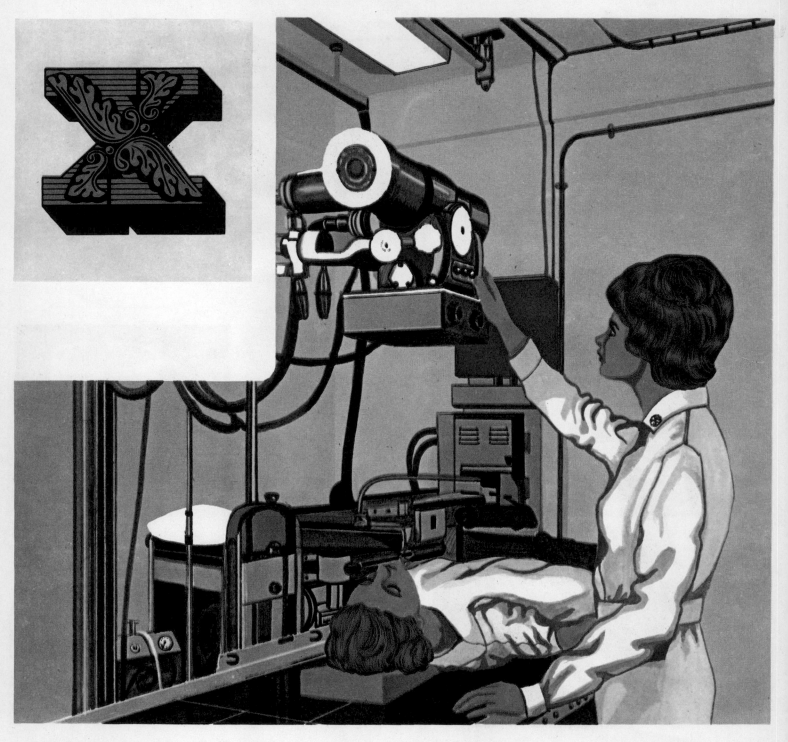

X-RAY By the use of X-rays which can photograph the inside of human bodies, doctors are able to see what is wrong with people.

XYLOPHONE This is a musical instrument made up of wooden bars which are struck by 'hammers' to produce a musical sound.

YACHT This is a light sailing vessel used for racing.

YAK This long-haired wild or domesticated ox of Tibet is used as a beast of burden.

YAM The yam is an edible tuber of a tropical climbing plant.

ZOO This is where animals are kept so that people can go and view them.

ZEBRA CROSSING To cross the road safely you should go to the Zebra crossing. These are black and white stripes painted across roads. At each side is a yellow lamp at the top of a pole which is called a belisha beacon.

ZEBRA This animal resembles a horse except of course that it has black and white stripes.

ION CREANGĂ PUBLISHING HOUSE
BUCHAREST

1984

Title of the original edition
Primul meu dicţionar
Editura Ion Creangă, Bucureşti

●

Editor MARIETA NICOLAU-PLĂMĂDEALĂ
Layout KLARA GALIUC